Made for His Glory

A Recovery Journey

BOOK ONE
Facing the Truth

Written by
Sharon Coletta

*Bring all who claim me as their God, for I have
made them for my glory. It was I who created them.
(Isaiah 43:7 NLT)*

Dedication

This program is dedicated to the many men, women, and children who will encounter God through this book, recovering that which was lost. God came to rescue and redeem us from death so we can live out our lives on earth according to our royal destiny with righteousness, peace, and joy, bringing us into His glory (Hebrews 2:10). This curriculum came

From Him while in corporate church prayer on January 3, 2023,

Through Him for the precious people of the earth who will be multiplied and repurposed, bearing much fruit,

To Him for His glory (Romans 11:36).

He was supreme in the beginning and—leading the resurrection parade—he is supreme in the end. From beginning to end he's there, towering far above everything, everyone. So spacious is he, so expansive, that everything of God finds its proper place in him without crowding. Not only that, but all the broken and dislocated pieces of the universe—people and things, animals, and atoms—get properly fixed and fit together in vibrant harmonies, all because of his death, his blood that poured down from the cross. (Colossians 1:18-20 MSG)

Table of Contents

My Story of Recovery

I have always believed in a God who was bigger than this world, and I always wanted to please Him, even when I had no idea who He was. Being raised in a big Catholic family who went to church every week, I was in awe of this God who didn't seem too interested in us. He was holy, and we were not.

As a very young girl, I begged my parents to wake me up early before school so I could attend mass at 6:30 a.m. I loved being in His house; I suppose I was seeking Him. In 1985, when I was 21 years old, I read a book on a plane by a Christian missionary who carried a cross throughout the world, preaching about Jesus. It was then that I asked Jesus into my heart. He flooded my soul, and I was never the same. Everything was new.

I eventually became part of a local church that preached the complete gospel, and I even went to Bible school. However, I carried with me old patterns of toxic, fear-driven, legalistic thinking and behaviors ruled by self-preservation. They didn't seem to go away even though I went to church and Bible school, read my Bible, prayed, volunteered, and attended church activities. Perhaps I thought it was just my personality type.

Eventually, I married a wonderful and stable Christian man, and we had a miracle baby girl, who is the love of our lives. Unfortunately, we were unable to grow our family anymore, which sent me into depression. The only dream I could distinguish that I had was denied. That was what brought me into the world of recovery, for which I am forever grateful.

It was incredible what I learned in recovery through the many tears and grueling honesty. In recovery, I received revelation about my toxic thinking and experiences as the Holy Spirit poured His love into my soul. I simply could not wear my Christianity on top of the turmoil within. When I stepped into reality, I needed to face the truth and accept responsibility for my poor behavior. I had developed toxic ways of coping in many relationships, and Jesus was replacing these coping mechanisms with His love, truth, and security.

The entire process brought so much freedom! His love for me is beyond anything I ever guessed I could experience. His presence in my life grows day by day, and the joy I now have in the midst of very painful and potentially debilitating circumstances is shocking. My day is a constant yielding and laying down of the self-effort I struggled with for years. When I was led outwardly, reacting to circumstances and people instead of being led inwardly by the Holy Spirit, I could not understand my own heart.

As I healed, I was honored to lead recovery groups and work with young teenagers in a local shelter. These precious people are my heroes! Many of them chose the same difficult, courageous journey of healing that I took. What an incredible generation of men and women, raised in chaos and brokenness, who do the seemingly impossible: finding love, joy, and purpose in God. The determination of this generation to be free from rejection, abuse, abandonment, and brokenness, as well as the self-destruction that comes from such life experiences, is breathtaking. Making releasing and grieving a discipline in their lives, their souls detangled and disengaged from the pain and unforgiveness that tried dominating and wrapping itself around them. What a Savior we have in Jesus!

I see a generation, young and old, that is rebuilding the old ruins, repairing the ruined cities (the desolations of many generations), and becoming trees of righteousness (Isaiah 61:3-4). Our God can do anything! I was completely wrong when I thought as a young girl that He wasn't interested in our lives. It is the opposite! His heart is completely invested in giving everything He has to see us be healed, whole, repurposed, and sitting at His royal table of abundant life! And this generation is going to see and do it!

Introduction

The purpose of this recovery journey is not to master the material but to connect with your Creator, God, in a personal way. He is the lover of your soul. He is not your problem; He is your solution. This is written with loads of Scripture, not for theological or doctrinal purposes but so participants are transformed by the true nature of God found in His Word. As you go through this workbook, you will gain a hunger for His written Word because the Bible is His love letter to you, His child. He spent everything precious to Him to purchase you back from darkness. He is so good!

Of course, this is written as a recovery program, but feel free to use it as a devotional or in a small group. However, the structure of a recovery program facilitates the optimum environment for participants to encounter God, find freedom through transparency, be known and seen, and be planted in His loving home—His church.

As you go through the lessons, do not be overwhelmed with the information. Allow God to speak to you through the process. Some lessons will speak more directly to you than others. Each builds on the other, so read them in order. Anyone who has been through a recovery program knows that you simply have to trust the process even when it becomes painful or confusing. Allow the Lord to bring truth to you, no matter how painful, because "you shall know the truth, and the truth shall make you free" (John 8:32). The truth is not always comfortable, but indeed, it is freeing!

The many questions, meditations, activities, and encounters are here so you can connect with God directly. As we get to know Him, we find that He is not really who we thought He was. He's way better. He can do way more, loves us more, and holds more power than we thought! Don't you want the real thing? He is absolutely invested in you, and He's for you—more than you are for yourself! He is available to reveal Himself and change our lives into the glorious one He planned before we were born!

Expectations and Group Overview

Welcome to a process that will open a new way of thinking and living as a child of God! Today is the day you courageously begin the process of discovering your true identity, who God made you to be. Through this workbook, you will learn at a deep level that

- Not only did God create you in His image, but He created you exactly the way He likes you. You are, in fact, made for His glory.
- God is not your problem; He's your solution.
- You are secure in His hands, and He won't let you go.
- Your failures don't change His love for you.
- You have been chosen, accepted, and called to a destiny and a purpose in this life. Jesus is never willing to back off His perfect plan for you.
- You hear His voice yourself because He is in relationship with you.

What Is Recovery? Recovery is "the act of regaining, retaking, or obtaining possession of anything lost."[1] When we use the word "recovery" in this workbook, it refers to the regaining of our original identity, position, purpose, and relationship with our Creator, God. This is expressed in three ways.

1. Through God, the Father, we are His child.
2. Through His Son, Jesus Christ, our Savior, we are given a free gift of forgiveness and righteousness to be His friend.
3. Through the Holy Spirit on earth, we can walk with God every day in His unfailing love, partnering with Him in what He is doing.

What Do I Need for This Group? An open heart, courage, and honesty. This group requires you to be honest before God and yourself. Once you are comfortable, you will become honest with others in a safe and secure environment. You will find relief to finally be honest—much like a dam that is released—and can now let healing waters flow. You will be required to purchase each workbook.

[1] *Webster's Dictionary 1828 - Recovery.* Webster's Dictionary 1828.

What Can I Expect to Get Out of This Group? By the end of this program, the expectation is that each person will

- Hear the voice of God for themselves.
- Experience an internal connection with God and others in a new way.
- Learn to offer themselves and others the free gift of forgiveness, kindness, respect, and honor as they experience and receive this dignity from God.
- Develop an inner peace that remains steady and secure even when life's circumstances are difficult.
- Have a renewed sense of purpose, destiny, and vision for their life.

How Long Is This Class? We will meet for two hours each week for up to nine months. The expectation is 100% attendance unless there is an emergency or sickness; therefore, think it through before committing. This may seem like a long time, especially in the beginning, which is the most difficult; however, you will find that the transformation in you is worth the investment. You will find yourself calm and secure, with patience possessing your soul, as Jesus said (Luke 21:19).

Life-Altering Decisions. During the length of this program, avoid making life-altering decisions, including marriage, divorce, change of career, moving far away, etc. You may find that your relationships, in general, will organically undergo changes as you change. Some relationships will improve, and some may be disengaged.

Guidelines for Participants

Safe and Structured Environment. To maintain respect in the group, we will follow certain guidelines also used in twelve-step programs because respect, dignity, and free will are foundational principles of the group.

- As you share, focus on your thoughts and feelings. You can tell a story that includes the behaviors of others while staying focused on yourself. Do not speak in generalities or preach to the group—be specific about yourself when you share.

- Each person is free to express his or her thoughts or feelings without interruptions. Therefore, there is no need to respond to anyone when they speak, except to thank them for sharing. We do not step into another's moment of truth when the Holy Spirit is revealing something. Avoid comforting another during class so that we do not interfere with their experience and revelation of truth.

- We are here to support one another, not "fix" one another. The Holy Spirit is the One doing all the fixing. Our job is simply to support each other's personal journey with their Creator while allowing the Holy Spirit to access our heart.

- Anonymity and confidentiality are basic requirements. If we find you are discussing anything outside the group, you will be asked to leave.
  - The only exception is when someone is in danger or harm, where steps must be taken to secure personal safety.
  - We only share another's testimony when they have shared it publicly.

- Avoid using foul language or extremely detailed descriptions of physical or emotional abuse or encounters so that you do not trigger others in the group.

Lesson 1
God Loves Family

Then God said, "Let Us make man in Our image, according to Our likeness; let them have dominion over the fish of the sea, over the birds of the air, and over the cattle, over all the earth and over every creeping thing that creeps on the earth." So, God created man in His *own* image; in the image of God, He created him; male and female He created them. Then God blessed them, and God said to them, "Be fruitful and multiply; fill the earth and subdue it; have dominion over the fish of the sea, over the birds of the air, and over every living thing that moves on the earth." (Genesis 1:26-28)

God is love (1 John 4:7). Since love has a burning desire to give itself to the object of its love, He made people. God did not need people because He is perfectly whole within Himself, nor does God need to feed His ego by ruling over anyone. He simply wanted people. Conversely, we need God even though He does not need us. Our entire existence is reliant on Him in every way (Psalm 100:3). In His generosity, He made us in His image so we could dwell with Him. Because we are made in His image, we are given free will to make choices, including choosing Him. Adam and Eve were His first family. Adam walked with God every day, and they were friends.

God created family as a safe place wherein we can be loved, known, heard, and validated. In the secure atmosphere of family, we can mature and grow while caring for one another. He created us to dwell with each other as family, and He even puts the solitary in families (Psalm 68:6). In fact, the entire human race yearns for a good family or to belong to a loving group. If we don't have a strong foundation of family, we may feel overwhelmed in the world instead of knowing our place or having a vision for life. God's plan is for every person to be in a loving family so we can see the world from a place of security, strength, vision, and destiny. We can then navigate the world with a sense of adventure and possibilities.

Where did we get this innate desire for family relationships? God put it inside us because we are made in His image: "God said, 'Let Us make man in Our image, after Our likeness'" (Genesis 1:26, emphasis added). God refers to Himself as "us" and "our." Our Creator identifies Himself within the Trinity, functioning in relationship. The Trinity includes the Father, His Son, Jesus, and the Holy Spirit (Matthew 28:19). He also chooses other rela-

-tional descriptions of Himself throughout the Bible, such as husband, friend, and brother. Here is a description of the roles of each member in the Godhead, or Trinity.

Father God is not just the lawgiver and judge; He is the head of the Godhead, who is our *protector* and *provider*.

> Father of the fatherless and protector of widows is God in his holy habitation.
>
> Psalm 68:5 ESV

> The LORD is my rock, my fortress, and my savior; my God is my rock, in whom I find protection. He is my shield, the power that saves me, and my place of safety.
>
> Psalm 18:2 NLT

> Do not fear, little flock, for it is your Father's good pleasure to give you the kingdom.
>
> Luke 12:32

Jesus Christ is not just the Son of God (Proverbs 30:4, John 1:14), our Savior, Prince of Peace, and King of Kings (Luke 1:31-33); He is also our *companion*, *brother*, and *friend*.

> The firstborn among many brothers and sisters.
>
> Romans 8:29 NLT

> No longer do I call you servants, for a servant does not know what his master is doing; but I have called you friends.
>
> John 15:15

> And suddenly a voice *came* from heaven, saying, "This is My beloved Son, in whom I am well pleased."
>
> Matthew 3:17

> But He answered and said to the one who told Him, "Who is My mother and who are My brothers?" And He stretched out His hand toward His disciples and said, "Here are My mother and My brothers! For whoever does the will of My Father in heaven is My brother and sister and mother."
>
> Matthew 12:48-50

The Holy Spirit is not just the Spirit of truth (John 16:13) and wisdom (Isaiah 11:2), but He is also our *miracle worker*, *comforter*, and *teacher*. Jesus sent the Holy Spirit so we are never alone or orphans.

> But the Helper, the Holy Spirit, whom the Father will send in My name, He will teach you all things, and bring to your remembrance all things that I said to you.
>
> John 14:26

> And I will pray the Father, and He will give you another Helper, that
> He may abide with you forever... I will not leave you orphans; I will
> come to you.
>
> John 14:16, 18

The Father, Son, and Holy Spirit are God in One, operating in unity at all times. They continue to support, confirm, share, and defer to each other. Because they are One, they can trust one another. Instead of control, they simply yield to and agree with one another. They are the example of a united family, operating as One. Look at how Jesus describes the Holy Spirit and how they all function as the Trinity.

> However, when He, the Spirit of truth, has come, He will guide you
> into all truth; for He will not speak on His own *authority*, but whatever
> He hears He will speak; and He will tell you things to come. He will
> glorify Me, for He will take of what is Mine and declare *it* to you.
> All things that the Father has are Mine. Therefore, I said that He will
> take of Mine and declare *it* to you.
>
> Romans 8:29 NLT

In John 5:16-30, Jesus describes the dependence and relationship between Himself and the Father, saying,

> The Son can do nothing by Himself, unless He sees the Father doing it.
> For whatever the Father does, the Son also does. The Father loves the
> Son and shows Him all He does… The Father judges no one, but has
> assigned all judgment to the Son.
>
> Romans 8:19-20, 22 BSB

When Jesus was accused of blasphemy, claiming deity by calling God His Father, He did not back down or apologize. He proceeded to describe the intimate relation between the Father and Himself to the point religious leaders wanted to kill Him. The Bible says that "He was even calling God His own Father, making Himself equal with God" (v. 18 BSB). Jesus boldly admitted, "I and *My* Father are one" (John 10:30). Jesus knew exactly who He was and His identity within the Trinity.

When God made us in His image, His desire was for us to be in His family, functioning in unity. When He made male and female (Genesis 1:27, Mark 10:6), He made it so that when they are joined together, they become one flesh in unity. Together He mandated them to be fruitful and multiply, filling the earth (Genesis 1:28) by having children. This is God's definition of family. It is the model He empowered to multiply and fill the earth. As a man and woman join and have children, they are equipped and empowered to be loving parents after the image of the Father. God's original design was not for any other institution, organization, or social setting to raise children. God chose family to provide what is necessary for children to flourish in health, growing into their destiny according to their identity, which was provided by their Creator before they were ever born on the earth (Jeremiah 1:5, Psalm 139:13).

Application

God created us because He loves us. He handcrafted us in our mother's womb, and no one controlled His decision to make you. (Jeremiah 1:5, Psalm 139:13-16). You were His decision. God simply cannot make junk because He is altogether good—He can do nothing less. Everything He makes is good, so He is never disappointed in what He creates. He even refers to His creation as very good (Genesis 1:31). We are uniquely made with various gifts, talents, and personalities after His image. Amazingly, He has not made any two people alike, including all eight billion people on the earth and the billions who went before us. Each person He makes is of the greatest value to Him, no exceptions! Each person is as special as the next, regardless of their experiences, location, or the work they do. Not only did He make us eternally valuable to Him, but He also intended us to view each other with that same incredible value. We are created to love one another, functioning together in family, relationship, and community after His likeness in the Trinity.

Although God created man and woman to be joined together as one flesh as a family, human beings simply cannot function as God intended without Him. So, we have varying family experiences that were not necessarily God's plan. Whatever our origin was, we learned a set of beliefs and internal messages that brought us to where we are now. With all the many countries, cultures, and belief systems, we developed a certain belief system from the time we were born—whether good or bad. As we move forward on this journey, we will assess where we've been and where we are now so we can begin the courageous process of moving forward, taking the good with us and moving toward God's original intent for our lives. This journey is absolutely freeing. Not only will you encounter the One who manufactured us, but we will also encounter the authentic and beautiful person He made us to be. You will like who you are because He does!

Now, let's look at our earthly family or place where we grew up and our experiences up to this point. We are simply assessing where we've been so we can begin the journey forward. Think of it as looking at a map. By locating where we are, we can move forward to the desired destination of peace. Our past journey or current location on the map may not be where we want to be. It could actually be a place of pain, abuse, broken relationships, or addictions. However, if we cannot locate it, we will continue to be disoriented, functioning in controlling habits, depression, anger, addictions, and isolation. When we suffer from behaviors and mindsets that rob our lives, we are unable to move forward into the abundant destiny God created us to live in. Let's begin this adventure!

Further Reading

Genesis 1:26-28	Proverbs 14:1	Luke 12:32	John 15:15
Genesis 2:18, 21-25	Proverbs 30:4	John 5:16-46	John 17:1-5
Proverbs 13:1	Matthew 3:17	John 8:13-36	Revelation 4:11

Discussion Questions

1. How would you describe yourself?

2. How did your family see God, the Creator, while growing up? Fearful? Loving? Disapproving? Accepting? Nonexistent?

3. How did your earthly father (or any other man) provide and protect your mother, siblings, and you? How was he unable to do this?

4. How did your earthly mother (or any other woman) encourage, nurture, and support your father, siblings, and you? How was she unable to do this?

5. As a child, where did you find acceptance and security?

6. What things in life make you feel accepted and secure now? What makes you feel unaccepted and insecure?

7. How do you handle pain and disappointment?

8. How do you protect yourself or cope through difficult situations?

9. What is the family "secret" God is asking you to face with Him (and possibly share with someone)?

10. How can you begin facing reality, leaving the secure place of denying the pain or problem?

Action Item: Declarations

Each day, speak these true statements and verses out loud, declaring them to your soul and agreeing with God!

1. <u>God Loves Me</u>.

I renounce the lie that I am unwanted or unloved.

I accept and declare the truth that God wanted me and made me the way He likes me.

He is very pleased with how He made me!

Then God saw everything that He had made, and indeed *it* was very good.

Genesis 1:31

For You formed my inward parts; you covered me in my mother's womb. I will praise You, for I am fearfully *and* wonderfully made; marvelous are Your works, and *that* my soul knows very well. My frame was not hidden from You, when I was made in secret, *and* skillfully wrought in the lowest parts of the earth.

Psalm 139:13-15

Before I formed you in the womb I knew you; before you were born I sanctified you; I ordained you.

Jeremiah 1:5

2. <u>God Chose Me</u>.

I renounce the lie that I am rejected by God.

I accept and declare the truth that He chooses and loves me.

Because the LORD loves you… the LORD has brought you out with a mighty hand, and redeemed you from the house of bondage.

Deuteronomy 7:8

The LORD your God in your midst, the Mighty One, will save; He will rejoice over you with gladness, He will quiet you with His love, He will rejoice over you with singing.

Zephaniah 3:17

As the Father loved Me, I also have loved you; abide in My love.

John 15:9

3. <u>God Created Me the Way He Likes Me</u>!

I reject the lie that I have no place in God's family.

I accept and declare the truth that God created me because He wanted me in His family.

And because you are sons, God has sent forth the Spirit of His Son into your hearts, crying out, "Abba, Father!" Therefore, you are no longer a slave but a son, and if a son, then an heir of God through Christ.

Galatians 4:6-7

Having predestined us to adoption as sons by Jesus Christ to Himself, according to the good pleasure of His will.

Ephesians 1:5-6

Behold what manner of love the Father has bestowed on us, that we should be called children of God.

1 John 3:1

Action Item: How I Describe Myself?

Write a brief overview of your life story up until this point. You can highlight the good as well as the bad. Invite God to help you tell your story. He is not angry or surprised, and most importantly, He was there with you the whole time, so He knows it. He will also guide you on what is necessary to write at this time. There is no need for you to share this with anyone unless you would like to. Your story is mainly a dialogue between you and God, allowing yourself the freedom and security to face the events in your life, whether good, bad, happy, or hard. You will look at your life together with the One who loves you and made you. The only requirement is that you allow yourself to be honest with your Creator, who already understands everything. Before you begin, I recommend a prayer similar to this one:

> *Dear God, please give me the grace and courage to go on this truth-finding journey. Help me to face reality as you reveal it. Show me what I need to see, no matter how difficult it may be. Hold me when I feel unstable or insecure. Guide me in the right direction. In Jesus' name, amen.*

____

____

____

____

____

____

____

____

____

____

____

____

____

Encounter: Seeing the Day God Made You

God is always with us and available (Deuteronomy 31:8). We are never alone (Hebrews 13:5). He is always eager to help us whenever we ask Him anything with a sincere heart (Psalm 46:1). God talks to people, and He wants to talk to you today (John 10:27) because He loves you and made you! Set aside 15-45 minutes to meet with God.

Many of us have no idea how precious we are. We do not understand why or how God could love us because we don't like ourselves. We wish we were different—that we had a different personality or better skills, talents, or intelligence. We only see ourselves with a limited viewpoint: our own eyes. We wish we were in a different family, or we may even think that God made us with the wrong gender.

In this encounter with God, we will ask Him to show us how He created and chose us to be exactly who we are. He sees us through the lens of His finished and perfect work that Jesus provided us. He sees who He created us to be—someone dependent, empowered, and abiding in His goodness. Begin by praying something like this:

> *Dear God, You said that every time You made something, You called it good! Please show me what You saw when You decided to make me—Your intention and my identity. Thank You for showing me that You were pleased when You made me. I choose to agree that You wanted me exactly the way You made me. I choose to agree with whatever You choose. Amen.*

Close your eyes and picture the very day when one of a million sperm came together with one of a million eggs to create someone who was God's decision. God chose all your DNA and chromosomes to fashion you! No human has the power to make life except God; only He could decide to create you.

Do you see that moment? Do you see how the exact combination of sperm and egg had to come together at the exact moment to make an electrical spark? Life! No human could have done this no matter how smart they are. Only God!

As God shows you how He picked the exact combination to be you, look closely at how happy He was with His creation. He chose your perfect eyes, nose, skin, hair, and personality. He chose your smile, laughter, gifts, and voice. He chose whether you would be a boy or girl, and He loves His choice!

As He fashioned you, He gave you a purpose and destiny to match how you were fashioned. Embrace His happiness and let it become yours. Agree with Him and share in His joy over you (Zephaniah 3:17).

Write down anything you see, hear, or feel about the day you were created.

____

____

____

____

____

____

____

____

____

____

____

____

____

____

Lesson 2
Adam & Eve: Good and Evil

And the LORD God commanded him, "You may eat freely from every tree of the garden, but you must not eat from the tree of the knowledge of good and evil; for in the day that you eat of it, you will surely die." (Genesis 2:16-17)

Because God is love (and love looks to give [John 3:16]), God created mankind for the simple purpose of sharing a loving relationship with us. This is why God created Adam and Eve around 3,940 BC, for a relationship. Adam walked with God, and life was good. God gave free will to Adam and Eve, allowing them the choice to reciprocate love back to Him. If God controlled them, this love could never be returned freely. Mankind would never have the opportunity to experience true love, intimacy, and affection for God. They would simply be robots. This is why each person is offered free will from our Creator. We have the option to voluntarily love Him back. Although God is all-powerful, He does not control, coerce, or manipulate because that is contrary to His nature and ultimate expression of love, which is freedom. In offering us freedom, God is vulnerable to the rejection of His human creation, which He, in fact, experiences on a daily basis.

God told Adam to "be fruitful and multiply; fill the earth and subdue it" (Genesis 1:28). God's only requirement of Adam was "of the tree of the knowledge of good and evil you shall not eat, for in the day that you eat of it you shall surely die" (Genesis 2:17). God reserved that knowledge for Himself to determine what was good and what was evil. God knew Adam had no capacity to determine what was good and evil outside of the Creator, so God asked Adam to trust Him to determine what was good and evil. In truth, Adam and Eve only knew good up until this point because God is absolutely good.

But Adam and Eve believed a serpent, who was in the midst of the garden, over God's command. Thus, Adam and Eve betrayed God, with whom they had a relationship. They made a decision independent of God, following their ideas (suggested by the serpent) that went against God's instructions. By doing this, they determined good and evil apart from God, and for the first time in their lives, they experienced the ultimate pain: separation from their loving Creator. Furthermore, they changed lords, coming under the dominion of Satan (Romans 6:16). All humans after them were born with this same spiritual nature—separated from God, choosing their own way, and under the dominion of death. The Bible says:

> Therefore, just as through one man sin entered the world, and death through sin, and thus death spread to all men, because all sinned.
>
> Romans 5:12

> For all have sinned and fall short of the glory of God.
>
> Romans 3:23

Because God's love is not willing to let go so easily, and it never gives up (1 Corinthians 13:7), He began a plan to get His children back into a loving relationship with Him. Throughout history, He spoke to and through many men and women as it unfolded. His ultimate plan was to send His Son to redeem us back, even when we chose to live independently from God.

This is why Jesus came to earth, worked miracles, taught us how to live, suffered, died, and rose again—to win us back by paying the penalty of Adam's, Eve's, and our sin. Romans 6:23 explains this: "For the wages of sin *is* death, but the gift of God *is* eternal life in Christ Jesus our Lord." According to Romans 5:8, "God demonstrates His own love toward us, in that while we were still sinners, Christ died for us." The only qualification to receive eternal life is to call upon His name (Jesus) to save you. However, in order to ask for salvation, you have to admit you are a sinner and are simply unable to save yourself. When we admit we cannot live this life our own way and we need God, everything changes.

> If you confess with your mouth the Lord Jesus and believe in your heart that God has raised Him from the dead, you will be saved. For with the heart one believes unto righteousness, and with the mouth confession is made unto salvation.
>
> Romans 10:9-10

> For "everyone that calls on the name of the Lord will be saved."
>
> Romans 10:13 ESV

> For God so loved the world that He gave His only begotten Son, that whoever believes in Him should not perish but have everlasting life. For God did not send His Son into the world to condemn the world, but that the world through Him might be saved.
>
> John 3:16-17

Even though we are now in the family of God, we continually must choose, like Adam and Eve, to either agree with God or go our way independent of God. This is the Christian walk.

Application

Once we call upon the name of Jesus, who was raised from the dead, we become sons and daughters of the Creator of heaven and earth. When we received Jesus as our Savior, we chose to follow Him and begin a new life. Jesus is the solution to everything in our lives. We will now begin walking through life with Jesus living on the inside of us.

> Therefore, if anyone *is* in Christ, *he is* a new creation; old things have passed away; behold, all things have become new.
>
> 2 Corinthians 5:17

Even though our hearts are "new," our minds have old memories, and the outside (our bodies) may still look the same. Our lives can still have the same problems as before, but we will begin handling our problems differently and even experience healing through Jesus. Without Him, we are crushed and conquered by the world and sin. Yet once we accept Jesus and allow Him to reign, we are conquered by love and righteousness, and a new person begins to emerge. These are two altogether different experiences of conquering: one produces death, and the other produces life.

We begin experiencing a new peace as we allow God to conquer our hearts. God will speak to us and help us. The only thing that is required of us is to be honest with Him and to agree with what He says. We must decide God is good, and we are simply unable to determine good and evil outside of Him. We make the decision to seek truth, and we agree to come face to face with the God of truth and ourselves. It takes a lot of courage to face the truth, but God's love is right there with us. He saved us and will not let us go! God promises that if we know the truth, it will set us free (John 8:32). Be assured that He is not condemning us; He is setting us free.

God gives us a free will, as He gave Adam and Eve, to agree with Him or not. If we want to choose our thoughts above His, we are actually saying we know better than God, which is what Adam and Eve did. In doing so, we place ourselves out of God's protection and back under Satan's dominion. Let's make the decision to agree with God. *Can we choose to trust Him?*

What if we built a house with character and beautiful architecture, but it had a faulty foundation? What if it was furnished with incredible fixtures, furnit-

-ure, and materials but was built on sand? This would be an unreliable foundation. That house would develop cracks in the walls and floors, eventually crumbling. This house represents our lives. We certainly want to know they are built on the foundation of solid truth so they can withstand all the storms of life. Jesus said it this way:

> Therefore, whoever hears these sayings of Mine, and does them, I will liken him to a wise man who built his house on the rock: and the rain descended, the floods came, and the winds blew and beat on that house; and it did not fall, for it was founded on the rock. But everyone who hears these sayings of Mine, and does not do them, will be like a foolish man who built his house on the sand: and the rain descended, the floods came, and the winds blew and beat on that house; and it fell. And great was its fall.
>
> Matthew 7:24-27

Let's look at the foundation of our lives and what we actually believe. Beliefs determine our thoughts. Thoughts determine our emotions and decisions. Decisions determine our actions, future, and relationships. It matters that our belief system is built on a foundation of truth!

Further Reading

Genesis 3	John 8:31-32	Romans 10:3-4
Matthew 12:48-50	Romans 3:10-26	1 John 1:5
John 3:1-21	Romans 5:1, 12, 15-21	

Discussion Questions

1. How have your expectations of others and yourself been unrealistic?

2. How has trusting only in your feelings and emotions been unsuccessful?

3. In what areas in your life are you beginning to face reality?

4. Have you accepted Jesus into your heart and become a child of God? If so, write your story of when and how it happened. If not, what is keeping you from embracing Jesus as your Savior, allowing God to be your ultimate truth?

5. Since you have become a child of God, what in your life has changed? What has not changed that you'd like to?

6. Adam walked with God, and then he walked in darkness. In what ways are you walking in light after receiving Jesus as your Lord and Savior? In what ways are you still walking in darkness?

7. How has walking in darkness affected your relationships?

8. Are you ready to stop trying to fix yourself, allowing God to do what you are unable to do for yourself? What would that be?

9. In what ways have you chosen to serve yourself (your way) over God (His way)?

10. What areas in your life are built on solid rock, and what areas are not?

Action Item: Making Jesus Lord and Savior

This decision is not about a dutiful prayer to make sure we're safe from hell (although that is one benefit); this is about being introduced (or reintroduced) to the real Jesus Christ, who rose from the grave and conquered death. He loves you with pure motives, which some cannot truly understand. Many of us have met a false Jesus who was presented to us in spiritually evil places, "appearing" light, only to find out it was dark and not the true Jesus. Others were presented a false Jesus by the world's system and religious-sounding words. However, the real Jesus Christ, who conquered death and this world's system, would like to enter (or re-enter) our lives because He is good and has no darkness or impurity in Him at all (1 John 1:5).

<u>Prayer of Salvation</u>. If you have not received Jesus Christ as your Lord and Savior, you can do so right now. Below is a simple prayer you can say out loud, putting your heart behind the words and meaning what you say. If you would like to use your own words, please do so! Salvation is not about saying specific words. Salvation is knowing Jesus Christ died for your sins and rose from the grave—that He conquered death, hell, the grave, and all sin in the world. This is about choosing Him, believing with your heart, and confessing with your mouth that Jesus Christ is your Lord (Romans 10:9-10)!

Make the following declaration out loud to God and for your soul to hear.

Dear Lord Jesus, I believe in my heart that You, Jesus, are the Son of God. I believe that You died for my sins because I could not pay that debt. I believe You were raised from the dead for my salvation and justification. I am calling upon Your name, Jesus, and I receive the salvation You purchased for me. My ways have not worked, so I now fully trust Yours. I am committing to follow Your directions and to obey You. I will trust Your ways because I know You have the power to transform and deliver me from the false gods and beliefs that have not worked. I believe in my heart and now confess that You, Jesus, are now my Lord! I give my life to You. I want to know You, serve You, and receive Your Holy Spirit because I need Your power. I reject the power the world has offered. I renounce those ways and commit myself to You, separating myself from any dark path. Please consecrate me; make me strong, pure, and obedient. Amen (I agree).

Action Item: Renouncing Lordship of Any False Gods or Beliefs

Just as Adam and Eve came into agreement with Satan and rejected God's words, we may have also come into agreement with evil, false religions, or practices that oppose our Lord. We may have done it knowingly or unknowingly, or our parents may have done it knowingly or unknowingly.

In either case, Jesus gives free will to come to Him, rejecting all evil, dark, and false religions or practices. You may know right away, or you may need to take time to ask God if there is anything to renounce. There is no need to look for something if it is not there. You will know, and there is no obligation to make up something.

Now that you are His child, simply ask your loving Father if there is anything you need to renounce. He is not angry; He will help you. There is nothing to fear about asking your loving Father to show you this because He also gives you the choice to simply turn your back on evil. It's very simple, and no one has control over your choice to follow God.

Dear Father, please show me anything I did, knowingly or unknowingly, that I must renounce to give my heart completely to You. I desire to give you my whole heart so that it is not divided. Amen.

Here is a list of things that may come to your mind.

Automatic Writing	Dungeons & Dragons
Astrology/Horoscopes	Eastern Practices for Spiritual
Bahaism	Development (Yoga, Zen, Martial
Blood Pacts/Cutting	Arts, etc.)
Bloody Mary	False (evil) Jesus
Buddhism	Fire Walking/Blowing
Card Laying/Tarot Cards	Fortune Telling
Chakras/Karma/Mantras	Ghosts/Ghost Hunting
Charlie Charlie/Ouija	Goddess Worship
Christian Science	Hare Krishna
Church of Scientology	Hinduism
Confucius	Islam
Crystals/Crystal Balls/Healing	Covens	Jehovah's Witnesses
Demons/Idols/Gods	Manifesting Abundance
Divination	Magic (White or Black)
Divining Rods	Mediums/Channeling
Dream Catchers	Mental Suggestions/Swapping Minds

<table>
<tr><td>

Mind Control
Nature Worship
New Age Medicine
Necromancy/Trances
Numerology
Paganism
Parapsychology Seminars
Pow-Wow Rituals (hot coals waved over sick)
Reincarnation
Roy Masters
Satanism/Satanic Rituals
Science of the Mind
Séances/Sorcery/Occult
Silva Mind Control
Shintoism
Shamanism
Spells/Curses/Charms
Spirit Guides
Table/Body Lifting
Taoism
Telepathy/Telekinesis
Totem Poles/Kachina Dolls
Transcendental Meditation
Unification Church
Unitarianism
Use of Omens
Violent/Horror/Sexual Video Games, TV, or Movies (including zombies/vampires)
Voodoo/Santeria
Witchcraft and Wicca
Willful Out-of-Body Experience

</td><td>

SECRET SOCIETIES:
Elks
KKK or Hate Groups
Masons/Freemasonry
Mormonism
DeMolay/Eastern Star
Shriners/Rainbow Girls
Job's Daughters
Tall Cedars
Daughters of the Nile
Knights of Columbus
Knights of _______________
Other _________________

</td></tr>
</table>

Then, simply say out loud:

I renounce _______________ in Jesus' name. Amen.

Lesson 3
Noah: God Saves and Delivers

By faith Noah, being divinely warned of things not yet seen, moved with godly fear, prepared an ark for the saving of his household, by which he condemned the world and became heir of the righteousness which is according to faith. (Hebrews 11:7)

Our God always makes a way of escape for His own, even if the whole world is against you! He is a Savior and Deliverer no matter how dark, impossible, and hopeless the situation is.

Noah was born around 2,885 BC, which was 1,056 years after Adam was created. Adam lived on the earth for 930 years and saw nine generations. There were few people that the Bible says *walked with God*. This included Adam (first generation), Enoch (seventh generation), and Noah (tenth generation). Noah (meaning "rest") walked with God (Genesis 6:9) even though the earth became filled with wickedness, corruption, and violence. Just as Adam relied upon himself instead of God, most of his offspring did the same, which only reduced mankind to levels of wickedness God never intended (Romans 7:18).

Throughout history we see how people without their Creator always become wicked, eventually destroying themselves. Yet Noah stood out and stood alone in a wicked society because he walked with God.

God said to Noah, "I will destroy man whom I have created from the face of the earth… The end of all flesh has come before Me" (Genesis 6:7, 13). But Noah found grace in the eyes of the Lord because he was a "just man, perfect in his generations" (Genesis 6:9). God instructed Noah to build an ark, which He ultimately used to preserve Noah, his family, and two of every animal that entered the ark. Every other living thing in the world drowned in the great flood.

This ark is symbolic of Jesus Christ, our Savior and our Deliverer, who alone saves us from every evil that surrounds us (2 Timothy 4:18, Titus 2:14).

The great apostle Paul said, "Yes, we had the sentence of death in ourselves, that we should not trust in ourselves but in God who raises the dead, who delivered us from so great a death, and does deliver us; in whom we trust that He will still deliver us" (2 Corinthians 1:9-10, emphasis added).

Noah prepared the ark (three stories high) according to God's plan. It took many decades to build it. Finally, when Noah, his wife, and three sons with their wives (eight people in all) entered the ark, God shut the door (Genesis 7:16), securing Noah's family safely inside and away from destruction. Our God always makes a way to preserve His own and destroy the wicked (Psalm 37:18-20). When the rain stopped, God made a covenant with Noah.

1. <u>Covenant Between God and the Earth</u>. God said, "I will never again curse the ground for man's sake… nor will I again destroy every living thing as I have done" (Genesis 8:21). When God promised that He would never again curse the ground, He provided a guarantee with His promise: "I set My rainbow in the cloud, and it shall be for the sign of the covenant between Me and the earth" (Genesis 9:13). Rain became a way God watered the earth. From the beginning, we see God's true heart of love toward mankind. His heart was not to destroy men but to save them, eventually sending His Son into the world for their salvation. The rainbow reminds us of God's promise.

2. <u>Law of Seedtime and Harvest Renewed</u>. God renewed His original law of seedtime and harvest with Noah that He established at the creation of the earth, whereby whatever seed is sown in the ground will be reproduced on the earth (Genesis 4:26-29). God declared this assurance to Noah that "seedtime and harvest, cold and heat, winter and summer, and day and night shall not cease" (Genesis 8:22). Thousands of years later, Jesus taught that the kingdom of God is like a man who plants a seed in the ground, which produces grain that is harvested (Mark 4:26-29). All things begin with a seed and, when they are planted, eventually grow into something larger as they are watered.

3. <u>Be Fruitful, Multiply, and Cover the Earth</u>. God then gave Noah the same command to be fruitful and multiply (Genesis 9:7) as He gave Adam and Eve. He spoke these words to all who walked with God.

In fact, God continually commanded His people to cover the earth throu-
-ghout the Bible. This is God's original design for us. By implementing
the law of seedtime and harvest for His kingdom, we become fruitful.
And when we multiply, we cover the earth.

<u>Noah's Three Sons</u>. Noah had three sons who came out of the ark with him: Shem, Ham, and Japheth. After God miraculously delivered Noah and his family from death, Noah became drunk and naked in his newly planted vineyard. He was discovered by his son Ham, who dishonored his father when he saw his nakedness (Genesis 9:22). Ham brought shame to his father and summoned his brothers to the scene. Conversely, Shem and Japheth refused to dishonor their father with Ham, covering him with honor (Genesis 9:22-23). In return, Noah blessed Shem and Japheth and cursed Canaan (Ham's son). He declared that Canaan would be a slave to Shem, and Japheth would dwell in tents with Shem (Genesis 9:25-27).

Noah's family began populating the entire earth, just as God commanded. Every person and nation on the earth today came from Shem, Ham, or Japheth (Genesis 9:19). The third generation of Shem was Eber. Six generations after Eber was Abraham, who was the first generation to be called Hebrews (meaning "sons of Eber"). Noah lived 950 years and saw ten generations after him. Shem lived 602 years and saw 12 generations after him.

Through the Hebrews, God gave a promise to His people all over the world that they would eventually be partakers of His covenant through Abraham, including those who are grafted in through Jesus Christ (Romans 11:17).

> For this is like the waters of Noah to Me; for as I have sworn that the waters of Noah would no longer cover the earth, so have I sworn that I would not be angry with you, nor rebuke you.
>
> Isaiah 54:9-10

Furthermore, all God's anger fell on Jesus as He hung on the cross and took our punishment. Therefore, we can be secure that He is no longer angry with us. He always finds a way to deliver and save us when we call upon Him!

Application

God is never trapped, bound, or cornered without a way out and through! Nor is He ever coerced to destroy His people simply because they are surrounded by darkness and wickedness. Never. He will secure us safely, just as He secured Noah's family in the ark, because we are hidden in God (Colossians 3:3). God has a million ways to get us to safety and His destination regardless of how impossible it seems—regardless of our origins, what we have done, our heritage, our circumstances, or our location. God makes a way where there is no way (Isaiah 43:16-19)! He is our Deliverer and Savior because we simply cannot save ourselves.

In the previous lesson, a curse came on the earth when Adam heeded the voice of his wife (Genesis 3:17) instead of protecting her and heeding the words of God. In the story of Noah, there was another breakdown in the family relationship—the father and son relationship between Noah and Ham. Noah and his three sons all made different decisions, and in doing so, they all sowed different seeds. As a result, they reaped different harvests. Noah unfortunately cursed his son because Ham violated and dishonored him. Ham then reaped a curse (Genesis 9:25) because he dishonored his father. Shem and Japheth reaped a blessing (Genesis 9:26-27) because of their choice to honor their father.

God loves family! In this lesson, it's vital for us to see how God requires us to honor our parents and parents to bless their children. If we sit in judgement over our parents, we are vulnerable to inviting a curse. God commands us to "honor your father and mother… that it may be well with you and you may live long on the earth" (Ephesians 6:2-3).If we honor our parents, we are blessed, and if we do not, it simply will not go well with us. If we have dishonored our parents and are now in Christ, we can turn from that path and thank Jesus, who redeemed us from the curse (Galatians 3:13). Even if our parents have done very wrong things, God asks us to honor them, as Shem and Japheth did, and not hate them in our hearts. God does not ask us to approve of evil behavior, but we are to honor the leadership that was placed over us.

There is tremendous hope for the future generations because God gave us

His remedy (Jesus) to restore broken family relationships. He showed us His heart of restoration in the very last verse in the Old Testament: "And he will turn the hearts of the fathers to the children, and the hearts of the children to their fathers" (Malachi 4:5-6). God repeated this prophetic word in the beginning of the New Testament. It was given in reference to John the Baptist and how he would be used to turn the hearts of fathers to their children (Luke 1:17) in preparation for the Savior. Jesus said there was no greater prophet than John the Baptist, and it was he, as Jesus' forerunner, that began restoring fathers and children. God loves our families, and He knows how to heal us and any broken relationships. God is the great Deliverer, Restorer, and Rebuilder!

Further Reading

Genesis 6-9	Psalm 91	2 Timothy 4:18
Psalm 34	Isaiah 43	2 Peter 2:5, 9
Psalm 37	Galatians 1:4	

Discussion Questions

1. In what ways were you pressured to follow the crowd, doing something you regret? In what ways did you take a stand, doing the right thing even when others did not?

2. Do you feel you need to protect yourself, or do you believe God can protect you?

3. What do you have control over? What do you not?

4. Do you feel obligated and driven to rescue others even if they put no effort into helping themselves?

5. Have you blamed someone else for your poor decisions?

6. How has God rescued you when you didn't see any way out?

7. Is there a pattern of rejections in your life?
   What does Psalm 27:10 mean to you?
   What does 1 Peter 2:4 mean to you?
   What does Galatians 1:15 mean to you?
   What does Ephesians 1:6 mean to you?

8. In what areas of your life are you ready to let God help and rescue you?

9. How have pain and rejection driven you to isolate?

10. What areas of life have you thought of yourself (survival) and not others?

Action Item: Declarations

Each day, speak these true statements and verses out loud, declaring them to your soul, the devil, and God, with whom you are agreeing!

1. I renounce the lie that I'm trapped with no way out.

   I accept the truth that there is no trouble God is unable to deliver me from (Psalm 34).

   The righteous cry out, and the LORD hears, and delivers them out of all their troubles.

   Psalm 34:17

2. I renounce the lie that people's persecution can stop the work of God in my life.

   I accept the truth that nothing God promises is impossible (Luke 1:37).

   Who shall bring a charge against God's elect? *It is* God who justifies. *Who is* he who condemns? *It is* Christ who died, and furthermore is also risen, who is even at the right hand of God, who also makes intercession for us. Who shall separate us from the love of Christ? *Shall* tribulation, or distress, or persecution, or famine, or nakedness, or peril, or sword?

   Romans 8:33-35

3. I renounce the lie that my sin is too great for God to deliver me.

   I accept the truth that nothing can separate me from God's love.

   Yet in all these things we are more than conquerors through Him who loved us. For I am persuaded that neither death nor life, nor angels nor principalities nor powers, nor things present nor things to come, nor height nor depth, nor any other created thing, shall be able to separate us from the love of God which is in Christ Jesus our Lord.

   Romans 8:37-39

4. I renounce the lie that ____
   I accept the truth that ____

   Scripture: ____

   ____

5. I renounce the lie that ____
   I accept the truth that ____

   Scripture: ____

   ____

Encounter: God Has a Way of Escape

God is always with us and available (Deuteronomy 31:8). We are never alone (Hebrews 13:5). He is always eager to help us whenever we ask Him anything with a sincere heart (Psalm 46:1). God wants to talk to you today (John 10:27) because He loves you and made you! Set aside 15-45 minutes to meet with God.

Just as God preserved Noah through the ark, a type of Jesus Christ, let's ask God to show us how our lives have been preserved even when we didn't see Him. We want to know where Jesus was when we were in danger, understanding how He never left us alone. Many of us have been in very dangerous situations, even surrounded by wickedness like Noah. And yet, God preserved us just as He preserved Noah.

Pray something like this using your own words.

Dear Jesus, I reject the temptation to ask You why something bad happened in my life. Instead, please show me Your heart and how You cared for me throughout my life when I didn't realize it. I trust You to show me how You rescued me. Amen.

As we ask God to show us where He was when we were surrounded by wickedness, we will find that He was right there with us. He never authored any abuse, rejection, neglect, or trauma we experienced because there is no evil or darkness in Him (Psalm 92:15, 1 John 1:5), nor does He author evil to accomplish His will (James 1:13). Of course, this world is filled with evil because He gave humans free choice, and Satan always tempts humans to do evil. When we were in danger or pain, He felt it and was working on a plan to deliver and set us in safety (Psalm 40:2). He brought us this far so we can begin a new life. Write down your thoughts that He shares with you

____

____

____

____

____

Encounter: Facing the Truth and Letting Go of Denial

God is always with us and available. We are never alone (Psalm 23:4, Hebrews 13:5). He is always eager to help us whenever we ask Him anything with a sincere heart. God wants to talk to you today (John 10:27) because He loves you and made you! Set aside 15-45 minutes to meet with God.

It is very easy to refuse to face the truth of our wrongful behavior. Instead of repenting to God and our loved ones, we can curse them for exposing our faults when they simply want to help. Facing the truth of our wrongs and those that others imposed on us is the beginning of freedom, the place where we stop blaming (them or us) and start healing. In truth, some of us have even blamed ourselves for wrongs others did to us. This also is not facing the truth. We are not responsible for the actions of others when we had no part in their hurtful or wrong behaviors. However, our responsibility lies in our reactions to their wrongs. For example, Shem and Japheth responded honorably to their father, while Ham dishonored him.

Freedom begins when we know the truth and are willing to face it (John 8:32). Simultaneously, learning the truth can also be one of the most frightening things we will ever do. It may require us to let go of illusions we created to protect our hearts from pain. It could also be difficult when others have created illusions for us in order to control us or our emotions. We can form idealistic beliefs or lies about people, places, our past, or ourselves simply because the truth may be too emotionally difficult to face. We present our best life for the public to see. Some of us mistakenly think that faith and denial are the same things. They are not. Faith is always based on God's truth and His Word. Denial is based on believing a lie.

There comes a point when we must face and address the truth for the healing process to begin. We must realize that the only secure and successful way of facing the truth and letting go of denial is with and through Jesus. Before we allow God to expose truth, let's remember how good God is, and let Him refresh you with His love. As you close your eyes, meditate on some truths.

You are alive because He kept you alive.
You were rescued by the God of the universe because He loves you.
You were led into this place because He wants to free you.
His thoughts toward you are only good.
He created you for good works, which you will walk into.
You are not junk because He simply cannot make junk.
He is glorious, and you look just like your Father because you are made in His image.
There is nothing too big that He cannot sort out.
Nothing is impossible with Him.

Sing to Him and allow Him access to talk to you. Pray something like this:

Dear God, I know you love me and want to set me free more than I even want to be free. Thank You for pursuing and covering me with Your blanket of acceptance and honor. Because I want to be free, please come and help me face the truth of my wrongs and the wrongs others did to me. Because You are with me, I know I can face the truth and not look to anyone else to blame or hate. I can simply allow You to hold me as we face reality together. I also know the devil brings condemnation, but You bring truth with love, so I trust You to hold and protect me in the process. Amen.

Write down any thoughts that come to you. God is not fragile; He can handle whatever you would like to talk to Him about.

____

____

____

____

____

____

____

____

____

____

____

Lesson 4
God's Covenant with Abraham, the Father of Faith

I am Almighty God... I will make My covenant between Me and you, and will multiply you exceedingly... you shall be a father of many nations... I will make you exceedingly fruitful; and I will make nations of you, and kings shall come from you. And I will establish My covenant between Me and you and your descendants after you in their generations, for an everlasting covenant. (Genesis 17:1-8)

Abram was born between 1960 BC and 1948 BC and was the tenth generation after Noah. Abram was 58 years old when Noah died at the age of 950. The ten generations before him covered about 300 years, and once again the earth became evil. The natural progression of mankind has been corruption and evil ever since the fall of Adam and Eve. Yet God found a man (later known as Abraham) who would command his children after him, keeping the way of the Lord in righteousness and justice (Genesis 18:19). While Abram was 75 years old and living in Ur of the Chaldeans, the Lord said to him:

> Get out of your country, from your family and from your father's house, to a land that I will show you. I will make you a great nation; I will bless you and make your name great; and you shall be a blessing. I will bless those who bless you, and I will curse him who curses you; **and in you all the families of the earth shall be blessed**.
>
> Genesis 12:1-3, emphasis added

Not only did God promise to multiply Abram, but He promised that all the families of the earth would be blessed through him. God works through covenant. He made a covenant with Adam, Eve, and Noah that involved blessings and curses. God now made a covenant with Abram. In this promise, God asked Abram to separate himself from all he had ever known by leaving everything behind, including most of his relatives. As difficult as that must have been, Abram obeyed God and took his wife, Sarai, leaving his family and the country where he grew up to walk in covenant with God.

> By faith Abraham obeyed when he was called to go out of the place which he would receive as an inheritance. And he went out, not knowing where he was going. By faith he dwelt in the land of promise as *in* a foreign country, dwelling in tents with Isaac and Jacob, the heirs with him of the same promise; for he waited for the city which has foundations, whose builder and maker *is* God.
>
> Hebrews 11:8-10

Although God called Abram and Sarai out of a wicked country, they were not perfect people. However, God was not looking for perfect people. He was only looking for hearts that would follow Him so He could transform them through His covenants and promises. By leaving this wicked country, Abram and Sarai began a courageous journey of pioneering a new way of living and thinking. Abram thought God was leading him to another city. Little did he know, he would give birth to an entire nation never known on the earth, completely set apart from the wicked civilizations that existed thus far.

God cut a covenant with Abram and gave him many promises. When Abram was 85 years old and again at 99 years old, God promised him a son through Sarai, who was 75 years old. One of the signs of the covenant was that God changed Abram's name to Abraham (meaning "father of a multitude") and Sarai's name to Sarah (meaning "princess"). Abraham and Sarah's life was a long journey of faith, which was continually tested. Could God's promises truly come to pass when it looks impossible? As Abraham waited for God's promise of an heir, years passed with no child. There came a day when Sarah took matters into her own hands, giving her maid to Abraham so an heir would come through a surrogate birth. Although Abraham agreed to this, God did not need a surrogate child to accomplish His will. He meant what He said: "I will bless her [Sarah] and also give you a son by her" (Genesis 17:16).

Abraham also took matters into his own hands when he gave Sarah (on two occasions) to the king because he was under pressure and feared for his life. Instead of protecting his wife, he hid behind her, making her vulnerable to violation and jeopardizing God's promise. So, God Himself rescued Sarah by appearing to the king in a dream.

Each time Abraham or Sarah attempted to control the situation because it looked bleak, they only made matters worse. They did not yet understand that God was able and faithful to every word of His promises and covenants. They did not see that God is unable to break His covenant. All of heaven and earth relies upon the words of God. Once God makes a covenant, He does not forget it or change His mind. He always fulfills the commitments He makes!

In their journey, there came a point when they relinquished all their control and surrendered to God's promise alone, without their self-efforts. This produced incredible strength and resolve within their hearts to trust God.

> And not being weak in faith, he did not consider his own body, already dead (since he was about a hundred years old), and the deadness of Sarah's womb... but was strengthened in faith, giving glory to God, and being fully convinced that what He had promised He was also able to perform.
>
> Romans 4:19-21

> By faith Sarah herself also received strength to conceive seed, and she bore a child when she was past the age, because she judged Him faithful who had promised.
>
> Hebrews 11:11

Sarah remembered God's hand of protection when she saw how God rebuked kings for her sake when she was trafficked by her husband! When she began seeing a God who was relentless in keeping His promise to her, her faith grew in this unseen God. She became so resolved in her trust that she even obeyed Abraham, calling him lord without fear (1 Peter 3:6). Not only was her faith not in her self-effort anymore, but it wasn't even in her husband's good or bad decisions. Her faith was now in her God alone—the One who fought her battles and protected her like no one ever had, the One who alone would perform His covenant. Her trust was so strong that she submitted herself to a man who made foolish decisions, putting her in danger. She knew her life was not in her husband's hands but ultimately in God's.

As promised, Sarah gave birth to Isaac (meaning "laughter") when Abraham was 100 years old and Sarah was 90 years old. Indeed, he brought them much laughter after their very difficult pioneering journey of faith. Isaac grew and became a father to Jacob. Jacob had twelve sons, and, after 400 years, this family became the great nation of Israel. God watches over His Word! (Jeremiah 1:12).

Now the blessing of Abraham comes upon us because we are in Christ (Galatians 3:14), so we inherit his blessings as his heirs did. Like Abraham, God separates us, calls us to a destination, and transforms our very nature to be like Him while equipping us to do whatever He has created us to do.

Application

In this lesson, God is asking us to become pioneers with courageous hearts, separating ourselves from destructive patterns of living and thinking or destructive people who are unsafe and lead us into darkness. (However, God is not asking us to necessarily quit a marriage or job just because it is difficult. That is altogether different.) God is asking us to follow Him like Abraham and Sarah did as they left Ur, which was a place of darkness, for a new destination, even if we don't know exactly where that is. Abraham looked for a city whose builder and maker was God (Hebrews 11:10). He was searching for a new foundation for his life.

God is also asking us to trust Him with our hearts, believing His promises by faith because He is trustworthy. Most of us have experiences with people who were supposed to protect, provide for, nurture, or help us, but instead they let us down, hurt us, or even violated us. Because of these experiences, it can be very difficult to turn over trust. Transferring trust can feel impossible with people and even more so with God, who is invisible. Yet that is exactly what God is asking us to do: trust Him. We are asked to follow Abraham and Sarah's example, following an invisible God and His promises. Of course, we can see why they took matters into their own hands at times. I'm sure they had thoughts just like us.

"Did He really mean what He said?"
"What kind of God is this?"
"Did I mess things up too badly for Him to do what He originally wanted?"
"Is He really able to pull off the miraculous?"

They did not know it is absolutely impossible for God to lie (Hebrews 6:18). He is a covenant-keeping God. But as they journeyed away from wickedness into a new foundation for life, their faith grew to where they could abandon themselves for what He promised. Even if we have never been able to trust anyone before, God asks us to abandon ourselves to trust Him with our whole heart, watching and witnessing His faithfulness as a covenant-keeping God! The most incredible thing happens when we begin putting our trust in a faithful God. As Sarah, we find out how much He loves and protects us— even among kings. People no longer hold the same power for our future that we once thought. As Sarah is our example, we no longer feel trapped by our own or others' mistakes and poor behaviors. When we are free to trust God, we no longer fear the decisions of others, who simply are imperfect.

Further Reading

Genesis 12:1-7   Genesis 17:1-8   Romans 4:1-25

Genesis 13:14-17   Genesis 20:1-3   Hebrews 11:8-16

Genesis 15:5-6, 18-21   Genesis 22:17-18

Discussion Questions

1. What is God calling you out of that is difficult to leave?

2. What do you want God to do for you?

3. What things in your life are you doing repeatedly, expecting different results?

4. What areas in your life are you ready to give up control and hand over to God?

5. Do you believe God will do what He says?

6. What covenant or promise has God spoken to you? Do you have the courage to believe Him?

7. Who or what is God asking you to submit to? How does that require you to have faith?

8. Who takes care of you the best, and how?
_________ your parents
_________ God
_________ yourself
_________ your friends
_________ your gang
_________ your church
_________ your government
_________ other

9. What new thing is God asking you to embrace?

10. Do you have the courage to let go of the past and reach for the future that is unknown?

Action Item: Declarations

Each day, speak these true statements and verses out loud, declaring them to your soul, the devil, and God, with whom you are agreeing!

1. I renounce the lie that God is abandoning me.
   I believe and declare the truth that He will never let go of me (Hebrews 13:5).

2. I renounce the lie that I have no purpose in this life.
   I believe and declare the truth that I am God's workmanship, created for good works (Ephesians 2:10).

3. I renounce the lie that I must take care of myself because no one cares for me.
   I believe and declare the truth that God cut a covenant with me, and no one takes better care of me than God (Psalm 8, 9:9-10, 37:3-5)!

4. I renounce the lie that ____
   I believe and declare the truth that _______________________________
   ____
   Verse/Promise: ____
   ____

5. I renounce the lie that ____
   I believe and declare the truth that _______________________________
   ____
   Verse/Promise: ____
   ____

6. I renounce the lie that ____
   I believe and declare the truth that _______________________________
   ____
   Verse/Promise: ____
   ____

7. I renounce the lie that ____
   I believe and declare the truth that _______________________________
   ____
   Verse/Promise: ____
   ____

Encounter: Leaving Ur and Following God

God is always with us and available (Deuteronomy 31:8). We are never alone (Hebrews 13:5). He is always eager to help us whenever we ask Him anything with a sincere heart (Psalm 46:1). God wants to talk to you today (John 10:27) because He loves you and made you! Set aside 15-45 minutes to meet with God.

What place is God asking you to leave (either physically, emotionally, or behaviorally)? As God begins showing you, spend time meditating on what that would look like, counting the cost, formulating a plan to leave your "Ur," and taking steps to your promised land. Let's not be frustrated or angry if we do not yet have the strength to leave Ur or cannot stop an addiction today. Simply picture what that would look like.

<u>Note</u>: Sometimes we think we are supposed to leave a job, marriage, or situation; however, it may be us simply wanting to quit. Quitting is not the same as following God out of Ur.

<u>Step One</u>. Begin picturing yourself leaving the old pattern of destructive living and embracing the new vision God is formulating in your mind. Meditate on the possibilities. Acknowledge it may feel uncomfortable, and be ready to conquer the challenges. Set your mind and be resolved before taking the next step.

<u>Step Two</u>. Allow the Holy Spirit to help you formulate a plan to leave the past behind and embrace the new journey. If God is calling you forward, He will lead you one step at a time. If you are doing this to quit or avoid obeying God, you will not have the strength or peace of God's leading. The following are some examples of leaving Ur.

<u>Example #1: Avoiding Explosive Anger</u>. If you see the familiar look of rage or control in your family member's eyes, plan another reaction and scenario rather than the same one that occurs repeatedly. No longer will you try to control the situation or rationalize, engage, or pacify. There's no need to defend yourself or the angered person. Simply remove yourself from participating by disengaging from the routine explosion or fight. No

threats need to be spoken. Every new action begins in your thoughts. Write down your new action, plan, or pattern.

<u>Example #2: Avoiding Temptation</u>. If you are regularly tempted with an addiction or are triggered into anger or depression because of a certain place (grocery store aisle, neighborhood, group, party, internet, phone, etc.), make a plan to avoid this place. Plan a new routine or reaction. If your temptation is a result of being triggered to self-nurture or avoidance through sexual deviation, take a moment to create an alternative plan in the face of rejection, internal pain, or feelings of abandonment. See yourself react differently or choose a different route (place, event, group, or situation). Leave your phone in your car or remove it from your home. Every new action begins in your thoughts. Write out your escape plan.

<u>Example #3: Letting Go of Fear</u>. If you are regularly in fear of anything, begin to imagine that when fear screams at you, you refuse to obey because you now want to please someone bigger: God. Insult fear with your refusal of it because it is no longer your god. Fear has no real power over you—it's just illusions, lies, and images. You control your responses. Push fear aside and obey only your Lord, who is always with you. Imagine what you would do if you had no fear of death, people's opinions, failure, or the devil. What would life look like if you broke up with fear? What would life look like if you had courage and chose only the Lord? What if you did the opposite of what fear demands? Every new action begins in your thoughts. Write out what you will do now that fear has no control over you.

<u>Example #4: Letting Go of Control</u>. If you are regularly controlling outcomes because you have no trust in those around you, begin imagining what life would look like if you were free to only manage yourself, allowing other adults to manage their behaviors. What if you allowed those around you to make choices without you? What would happen if you were not everyone's savior? How freeing would it be to only control yourself, letting others reap their consequences? Can you allow your loved ones the freedom to fail? Every new action begins in your thoughts. Write out your escape on paper.

Pray something like this prayer once you have given thought about what you are leaving.

> *Dear heavenly Father, I see now that You are asking me to leave _______________________________ (fear, anger, addictions, enabling/controlling others' problems, an unhealthy community, etc.). Although this thing is sabotaging and draining me of living, I do not know another way to live. Please give me the courage and strength to leave this place, following You to where I have never been. I thank You that You promised You will always be with me. I choose to trust that You can take better care of me than I can of myself. I know the journey may not be easy, so I ask that You strengthen me along the way as I learn how to live a new way where You are, my Lord and God. Amen.*

Write out any thoughts God has shown you.

____

____

____

____

____

____

____

____

____

____

____

____

____

____

Lesson 5
Freedom from Slavery

But because the LORD loves you, and because He would keep the oath which He swore to your fathers, the LORD has brought you out with a mighty hand, and redeemed you from the house of bondage, from the hand of Pharaoh king of Egypt. (Deuteronomy 7:8)

Up until this point, we learned that God loves and wanted family; therefore, He created Adam and Eve. Unfortunately, Adam and Eve chose their way over God's. Their disobedience caused sin to be the natural default of all humans afterward. Evil permeated the earth, but God preserved Noah because he walked with God. God's love for His family is great, so He continued His plan to get His family back by entering covenant with Abraham and Sarah, then their son, Isaac, and his son, Jacob.

Jacob had 12 sons who became known as the Hebrews. Even though the Hebrew sons of Jacob were competitive, cruel, and very jealous (Genesis 34, 37), God was faithful to the covenant He made with Abraham, Isaac, and Jacob. God said that all the families of the earth would be blessed through them (Genesis 12:3, 28:14, Acts 3:25).

Joseph's Slavery. One day, one of the youngest of the 12 brothers, Joseph, shared two dreams with his older brothers. In these dreams his brothers all bowed down to him. This infuriated the brothers, so they found an opportunity to entrap Joseph, throw him in a pit, sell him as a slave, and lie to their father that a wild beast ate him. Joseph was betrayed, abandoned, naked on an auction block, sold, enslaved, falsely accused, imprisoned, chained, and forgotten for many years, but God was with him, and He declared that Joseph was a successful man (Genesis 39:2). Joseph carried an attitude of forgiveness wherever he went, as God directed his steps and blessed everything he did. While Joseph was imprisoned, he interpreted Pharaoh's dream, which led to him becoming second in command of Egypt. After many years, he was the one who preserved the entire nation, as well as his family, from a seven-year famine. Indeed, his brothers and father bowed down to him. In the process, Jacob and all his sons with their families (70 people in all) went to live in Egypt. As Jacob prepared to move to Egypt, God again made a covenant with him.

> I *am* God, the God of your father; do not fear to go down to Egypt, for I will make you a great nation there. I will go down with you to Egypt, and I will also surely bring you up *again*.
>
> Genesis 46:3-4

<u>Children of Israel's Slavery</u>. Of course, everything God promised is exactly what happened. After 430 years in Egypt, this Hebrew family grew to become a great Hebrew nation of about two to five million people (including men, women, and children). The Egyptians became jealous of them because they grew into such a large people group (more than the Egyptians) and prospered abundantly in the most fertile land of Goshen. While the Egyptians gradually enslaved them, nothing could stop God's promise to Abraham to give his descendants the promised land of Canaan. Therefore, God sent Moses to lead them out. He came to the children of Israel and gave them a message from God.

> **I have** also established My covenant with them, to give them the land of Canaan, the land of their pilgrimage, in which they were strangers. And I have heard the groaning of the children of Israel whom the Egyptians keep in bondage, and I have remembered my covenant. Therefore, say to the children of Israel: "*I am* the LORD; **I will** bring you out from under the burdens of the Egyptians, **I will** rescue you from their bondage, and **I will** redeem you with an outstretched arm and great judgments. **I will** take you as My people, and **I will** be your God. Then **you shall** know that *I am* the LORD your God who brings you out from under the burdens of the Egyptians. And **I will** bring you into the land which I swore to give Abraham, Isaac, and Jacob; and **I will** give it to you as a heritage: *I am* the Lord." So Moses spoke thus to the children of Israel; but they did not heed Moses, because of anguish of spirit and cruel bondage.
>
> Exodus 6:4-13, emphasis added

When Moses delivered the plan of freedom to the Hebrews, they could not believe it. God simply told them everything He was going to do for them; He was not asking them to do anything except to know it. Committed to His covenant with Abraham and his family, whom He loved, He was delivering them. Because the Hebrews didn't have any strength to believe Him, God brought them out with His strength (Exodus 13:3, 14, 15:2).

The deliverance from slavery in Egypt began when Moses gave God's message to Pharaoh multiple times: "Let My people go, that they may serve Me" (Exodus 7:16, 8:1, 8:20, 9:1, 9:13, 10:3). Never had any god in all the known world been that powerful, faithful, and benevolent to ensure the liberty and freedom of a whole people group. This was the birthing of His nation! God knew that when His people were freed, they could freely serve the True and Living God and receive His abundant promises. Just as God created Adam and Eve with the free will to reciprocate love back to their God, so God freed the Israelites so they could worship and minister to Him freely. He desired to make them a nation of priests (Exodus 19:6). God is a free God, and He is the One who frees us to worship and serve Him!

Application

How is it that Joseph's slavery appeared to be more severe than the children of Israel's, yet he prospered while the children of Israel's hearts became small or shrunk (as indicated above in Exodus 6:9, described as "anguish of spirit")? He had no family or friends with him. He was in a foreign land by himself, which meant he had to learn a new language and customs. He was even put in chains in a prison house (Psalm 105:17-18). Yet Joseph had favor and prospered. His masters trusted him, even relying upon him to oversee and manage the other servants, slaves, and prisoners. Joseph prospered wherever he went—even in prison. The other slaves under him were happy and productive, rarely sad (Genesis 40:6-7). How did Joseph function from a mindset of security and strength when so much evil happened to him? Psalm 105:17-19 (AMPC) gives us a hint.

> He sent a man before them, even Joseph, who was sold as a servant. His feet they hurt with fetters; he was laid in chains of iron *and* his soul entered into the iron, until his word [to his cruel brothers] came true, until the word of the Lord tried *and* tested him.

These words indicate that Joseph's soul became as strong as iron when he was in prison. He became fixed and strong in mind and heart with a resolve to believe God's words and God's faithfulness to him, regardless of what people did to and against him.

Contrast Joseph's experience of slavery with the children of Israel, who came from the exact same family of Jacob. They were given the promises passed down to them from their grandfather, Abraham, that they would become a great nation. Yet their experiences and responses to slavery were the opposite. How did their souls become filled with anguish while Joseph's soul was strengthened? Compared to Joseph, they held many benefits. They were able to dwell together as a family, so they were not alone like Joseph was. They were not betrayed and sold by their brothers like Joseph was. They did not need to learn a new language and could carry on with their known culture at home, unlike Joseph. They were fruitful, multiplying into a great nation, which most historians believe to be more in population than the Egyptians, their captors. God was blessing their health, wealth (animals), and posterity. What kept them from believing and trusting that God would do what He said? They could only see their impossible situation, somehow only believing they would be slaves and victims, unable to choose for themselves or experience freedom. Likewise, what is keeping us from believing and trusting that He will free us and keep His promises?

Unlike Joseph, who kept a dream in his heart (and forgave his brothers), the children of Israel forgot the promises given to their grandfathers about going down to Egypt, becoming a great nation, and coming back up to possess the land of Canaan. How could they forget? Did they settle into the good life of Egypt? Perhaps the span of four generations caused the promise to dim or seem like an old fable. Regardless of how it happened, by the fourth generation, they only knew slavery. As Egypt made them carry heavy burdens, we can only guess it became difficult to believe in God's goodness anymore, and, as a result, they felt an anguish of the soul. God had to get them back to a place that believed Him again.

Children can often carry their parent's negative attitudes in their soul, such as fear, guilt, or shame, without necessarily experiencing the same event that caused it. Of course, these mindsets would make believing in miracles difficult. Guilt and shame are extremely heavy burdens for anyone to carry. They are toxic to the soul, convincing us that God is angry with us or that He is unable or unwilling to be good to us. Furthermore, guilt and shame are the ultimate lies we believe that keep us from connecting in relationship with Him, ourselves, and the very people we love.

When we compare the two stories, we have to wonder—does freedom originate from within our soul, or does it originate outside us from our circumstances, our station in life, or the permission of others? Do we need to hear God for ourselves instead of stories from others' experiences? Can internal freedom produce external freedom? Is God able to produce both for us? How do we see ourselves? Can our Creator free us if we believe Him, and if so, how can we have confidence in God's promise when life is difficult? Absolutely, God rescues and calls us out from our confinements (addictions, abuse, shame, depression, abandonment, persecution, etc.). As He delivers us, do we have enough strength to leave our prison and walk into freedom? Here's what God says to us:

> Christ has set us free to live a free life. So take your stand! Never again let anyone put a harness of slavery on you.
>
> Galatians 5:1 MSG

Further Reading

Genesis 37, 39-41	Psalm 105	John 8:35
Genesis 45:7-8	Luke 4:18	Galatians 2:4, 4:7, 5:1
Exodus 3:7-10, 13:3, 14	John 6:37	2 Timothy 2:13

Discussion Questions

1. What do you want God to free you from?

2. What has God promised you directly? Do you believe Him?

3. What regret do you carry that is keeping you from experiencing God's freedom?

4. How have you learned to survive and only trust yourself over God or others?

5. How have you regrettably persecuted others because of your jealousy, bitterness, rebellion, or hatred?

6. What shame or guilt are you holding onto that keeps you from experiencing God's care? What does John 6:37 mean to you?

7. What are you willing to turn over to God's care so He can help?

8. Now that you are in God's family and are a child of God, do you believe you will remain in His family forever? Or do you still think you will be kicked out of His family, like a slave, if you do something wrong? What does John 8:35 mean to you?

9. Why is it important for us to have support from family, friends, or other Christians?

10. How can we stay free from bondage? What does Galatians 5:1 mean to you?

Action Item: Declarations

Each day, speak these true statements and verses out loud, declaring them to your soul, the devil, and God, with whom you are agreeing!

1. I reject the lie that I will always be alone or in bondage.

   I accept the truth that God has released me from bondage, and I don't have to manage it anymore.

   I am no longer a slave but a son/daughter, and if I am a son/daughter, then I am an heir of God through Christ.

   Galatians 4:7

2. I reject the lie that I will always be controlled by random impulses.

   I accept the truth that God has supplied me with the power to overcome any addiction or bad habit.

   And because you belong to him, the power of the life-giving Spirit has freed you from the power of sin that leads to death.

   Romans 8:2 NLT

3. I reject the lie that I have to wander through life unsupported.

   I accept the truth that I have now been brought into God's family.

   Even before he made the world, God loved us and chose us in Christ to be holy and without fault in his eyes. God decided in advance to adopt us into his own family by bringing us to himself through Jesus Christ. This is what he wanted to do, and it gave him great pleasure.

   Ephesians 1:4-5 NLT

4. I renounce the lie that ______________________________________
   I accept the truth that ______________________________________

   Scripture: ______________________________________

   ____

5. I renounce the lie that ______________________________________
   I accept the truth that ______________________________________

   Scripture: ______________________________________

   ____

Encounter: Walking Out of Prison Doors and Becoming Untethered to the Past

God is always with us and available (Deuteronomy 31:8). We are never alone (Hebrews 13:5). He is always eager to help us whenever we ask Him anything with a sincere heart (Psalm 46:1). God wants to talk to you today (John 10:27) because He loves you and made you! Set aside 15-45 minutes to meet with God.

This encounter is an exercise in connecting to God and His promises, detaching from the past that we may feel tethered to. Have you ever played tetherball? You can hit a tetherball with all your strength, but it will simply bind itself tighter to the pole it's connected to. This is a picture of how we can be bound to something that we can't seem to get free from. Oftentimes, the harder we try and remove that thing, the tighter it binds us.

But just like God came and delivered the children of Israel from slavery into sonship with a mighty hand, Jesus has likewise set the captives free so we can serve Him (Luke 4:18) and be untethered to our past. He completely cut us off from the guilt and shame of it!

<u>Step One</u>. Quiet yourself, focusing on Jesus, your Savior and Friend, or Father God. (You can sing to Him about His goodness or pray and thank Him.)

<u>Step Two</u>. Ask the Father if there is any rope, chain, or prison cell keeping you tethered other than Him. You can pray something like this:

> *Dear Father, I desire to only be attached to You. Detach me from anything that is not from You. Please show me if there is anything in this world or in my heart that keeps me tethered to something other than You. My desire is to connect to You, Your plans, and Your people—free to be in full relationship with You as Your child. Thank You for hearing my prayer and for answering my questions. Amen.*

<u>Step Three</u>. Write down anything that comes into your mind or thoughts that He is telling you. His biggest desire is to see you free to be His. God is fully committed to showing you anything that keeps you from Him so that He can remove it at your request. He is not holding back!

Step Four. Once He shows you anything that is keeping you from connection with Him, you can pray something like this:

> *Dear Father, I break off* ______________________________,
> *which keeps me from being fully connected to You as Your child. In Jesus' name, I choose to walk out of this prison door of* ______________________________ *because You have already set me free according to Luke 4:18. You made me Your child because You wanted me in Your family. In Jesus' name, amen.*

In Jesus, we are no longer tethered to the past—we are only tethered to Him and the future He has for us. The following lessons will further strengthen this activation, encounter, and prayer.

Lesson 6
Ten Commandments: The Standard of God

The law of the LORD is perfect, converting the soul;
The testimony of the LORD is sure, making wise the simple;
The statutes of the LORD are right, rejoicing the heart;
The commandment of the LORD is pure, enlightening the eyes;
The fear of the LORD is clean, enduring forever;
The judgments of the LORD are true and righteous altogether. (Psalm 19:7-9)

God delivered His people, the children of Israel, from slavery because He was fulfilling His covenant to Abraham, Isaac, and Jacob. Remember, God wanted a family and relationship with men and women (including you and me), who are made in His image. Our mandate is to multiply and cover the earth.

God told Moses in Exodus 6:3 (KJV), "And I appeared unto Abraham, unto Isaac, and unto Jacob, by the name of God Almighty, but by my name JEHOVAH was I not known to them." God was now revealing Himself to the children of Israel in a new way. What does this mean? When God revealed Himself to Abraham, He cut covenant, fulfilling promises even when it seemed impossible. Now, God wanted to show His purity and holiness to those in the covenant of Abraham. However, there was a problem because man could not approach God's purity and light. No man could see God and live (Exodus 33:20). Therefore, as He revealed His holiness through the commandments, He also taught the covenant people how to approach Him through the temple so He could meet with them.

In His love, He prepared a way for His covenant people to converse with Him and serve Him on earth. He delivered and positioned them so they could meet with Him (Exodus 9:1). Three months after they were freed from Egypt, Moses spoke with God on Mount Sinai, where God gave an incredible message.

You have seen what I did to the Egyptians, and *how* I bore you on eagles' wings and brought you to Myself. Now therefore, if you will indeed obey My voice and keep My covenant, then you shall be a special treasure to Me above all people; for all the earth *is* Mine. And you shall be to Me a kingdom of priests and a holy nation.

Exodus 19:4-6

God was now requiring something from His people. He proceeded to deliver laws, standards, and ceremonies that this new nation must obey. He did this for their good, to preserve them (Deuteronomy 6:24). As God provided laws and governance to His covenant people, the Lord said to Moses, "Write these words, for according to these words I have made a covenant with you and with Israel" (Exodus 34:27). These laws are referred to as the Law or the Old Covenant, which includes the Ten Commandments.

1. Do not have other gods before Me.
2. Do not make or serve an idol. Do not bow down to them.
3. Do not take the name of God in vain.
4. Keep the Sabbath day holy.
5. Honor your father and your mother.
6. Do not murder.
7. Do not commit adultery.
8. Do not steal.
9. Do not bear false witness.
10. Do not covet anything your neighbor has.

See Exodus 20:1-17

It was vital for Moses to deliver every word to this new nation—a pure standard that set apart Jehovah's people. God asked the Israelites to come up to His standard of purity for living, unlike any nation that ever existed before in the world. He showed them a relational dignity that no people group had ever experienced. As God raised this standard, He knew full well that even His chosen people could never meet what is required for an intimate relationship with Him. Therefore, He also provided the ceremonial sacrifices and cleansing that covered their inability to keep the law—all so He could remain in fellowship with them. It was vital for a holy God to reveal His holiness because holiness simply could not dwell among sinfulness and lawlessness. It was His passionate desire that His people meet with Him. Up until this time, God did not reveal His unattainable nature of holiness or communicate His high standard of living to any people on the earth. Although God's standards were always the same, by revealing Himself as Jehovah, the people were responsible for meeting His standard for the first time. They were responsible for a code of moral ethics and behaviors because "sin is not imputed where there is no law" (Romans 5:13). Furthermore, God provided all the consequences for good or bad behavior in Deuteronomy 28, which includes all the blessings if they obeyed His law and curses if they did not.

Application

Imagine the earth filled with people and cultures where there was no unchangeable or consistent standard to determine what was good or bad. Where laws and rules were constantly changed, dependent on the opinion of others who dominated communities, states, and nations. What if truth, good, and evil were all changeable? This is relativism, which is "the belief that truth and right and wrong can only be judged in relation to other things and that nothing can be true or right in all situations."[2] If laws are relative, there is no ultimate standard of good or evil. With this being said, how do we discern truth?

For example, when is killing another person permissible or illegal? There are nuances to this, like killing in time of war, killing to defend ourselves or our family, killing a person in the womb, and killing the elderly if they are helpless, sick, or unproductive in society. Who decides who lives or dies? Furthermore, if we choose what is good or evil for ourselves, we become our own god, forming ideas from our limited understanding and emotional state, whatever that may be. This is exactly what Adam and Eve did in the garden as they chose who and what to believe when the serpent offered an alternative to God's word.

If we live out of our thoughts and desires, we will satisfy ourselves at all costs, even if it means violating others to get what we want and need. Furthermore, any good we do would simply be for the end goal of getting what we want or need. The volume of violations against one another would run rampant, and people would consume each other simply because there were no standards or rules of conduct with consequences and rewards. If this seems a bit radical to us, let's remember that when Adam and Eve ate from the forbidden fruit, sin entered the world. From that time on, civilization only spiraled downward for evil, as is evident from the story of Noah and when God called Abraham out of Ur of the Chaldeans. Throughout history, civilization only spirals to barbarianism without Jehovah God's standards showing us good from evil. This is how civilization functioned before God revealed Himself as Jehovah, and this is why we are now making a conscious decision to agree with God and all His standards and laws. He is Truth (John 14:17, 15:26, 16:13).

[2] "Relativism." *Cambridge Dictionary.*

Ultimately, God was saving humanity from themselves by revealing His vehement holiness through the law. Valuing Jehovah's commandments and laws would bring righteousness, consistency, morality, and expectation of consequences that remain consistent.

Later in Israel's history, we see King David was a man after God's own heart (Acts 13:22). Although he committed sins, he continually declared throughout Psalm 119 that God's laws and judgments are righteous and a delight. He never defended his sins as right but always chose to agree with God that His law was good and perfect no matter the cost. In fact, David said, "The law of the LORD *is* perfect, converting the soul" (Psalm 19:7).

Jesus sums up all the commandments and laws this way: "'You shall love the LORD your God with all your heart, with all your soul, and with all your mind.' This is *the* first and greatest commandment. And *the* second is like it: 'You shall love your neighbor as yourself. On these two commandments hang all the Law and the Prophets" (Matthew 22:37-40). Jesus further says, "If you love Me, you will keep My commandments" (John 14:21 ESV). Therefore, we can conclude that all God's commandments are motivated by His love for us. God's love is the fulfillment of the law: "Love makes it impossible to harm another, so love fulfills all that the law requires" (Romans 13:10 TPT).

The giving of the law and the revealing of Jehovah's vehement holiness were necessary to bring us closer to God as mankind waited for His holy agenda to be revealed and fulfilled on the earth. Therefore, for this lesson, let's not be overwhelmed if we do not keep all God's commandments. For now, simply agree with God that His commandments are good, and we love His law. Romans 7:16 (NLT) says, "But if I know that what I am doing is wrong, this shows that I agree that the law is good." The result is peace: "Great peace have those who love Your law, and nothing causes them to stumble" (Psalm 119:165)!

Further Reading

Exodus 33-34	Matthew 22:34-40	John 15:10
Deuteronomy 5-8, 28, 30	Mark 22:28-30	Romans 7:16-25
Psalm 119	John 5:44	Romans 8:1-4
	John 14:15, 21	

Discussion Questions

1. Is there any standard in your life God is asking you to raise?

2. Do you remember a time when something felt so true to you, but you learned it was not true, and you were simply deceived?

3. Have you ever humbled yourself and agreed with God even when it cost you something? When and how?

4. What law of God are you violating that you would like to change?

5. What beliefs have you let go of when you learned God's standard and made a decision to agree with Him?

6. What beliefs are you having difficulty letting go of to agree with God? Why?

7. Are you afraid to ask God His opinion on any situation in your life? Why are you afraid to choose His thoughts?

8. List the things you have used to block the pain of your past.

9. Do you have wrongdoing for which you carry guilt?

10. Currently, who is the most important person or thing you want to please in your life? Truthfully number the top five in order of importance.

    a. Your parents
    b. Your priest/pastor
    c. Your spouse
    d. Yourself
    e. God
    f. Your children
    g. The government
    h. Your boss
    i. Your customers
    j. Your followers
    k. The crowd
    l. Your schoolmates
    m. Your political party
    n. Your ministry
    o. Your church
    p. Anything else

Encounter: Being Responsible for Me

God is always with us and available (Deuteronomy 31:8). We are never alone (Hebrews 13:5). He is always eager to help us whenever we ask Him anything with a sincere heart (Psalm 46:1). God wants to talk to you today (John 10:27) because He loves you and made you! Set aside 15-45 minutes to meet with God.

We come into this world as a helpless little baby unable to survive without another person taking responsibility for us. As we grow into adulthood, we become increasingly responsible for our behavior, decisions, and responses to others' behaviors and decisions that affect us. Many times we want to depend upon someone else making decisions for us because it's easier and less stressful. In doing so, we don't have to grow up. We can always blame someone else when bad things happen. Much of the time we simply don't want the responsibility of choosing our life. We often lack courage, and we would rather be taken care of, regardless of the source.

Just as God set the nation of Israel free from slavery so they could serve Him, He set us free from our past sins so we can freely serve Him. He gave us His standard of living so we could make good decisions in our lives, preserving us (Deuteronomy 6:24). We no longer can blame God or others for our poor decisions. This doesn't mean that we must be perfect or that we are always to blame when something goes wrong. It simply means that He's available and will help, lead, and guide us. To do this, He gave us His Word, which is a lamp to our feet and light to our path (Psalm 119:105).

Therefore, God wants us to depend on Him first and not overly depend on others for His guidance. (Note: There is a healthy dependence in our relationships with others, which we will look at in future lessons.) Because God was teaching Joshua and the nation of Israel to depend on Him instead of any government, He told them, "This Book of the Law shall not depart from your mouth, but you shall meditate in it day and night, that you may observe to do according to all that is written in it. For then you will make your way prosperous, and then you will have good success" (Joshua 1:8).

God's Word gives us the ability to make good decisions and prosper. Life won't be perfect, but we can follow Him regardless of our circumstances. He's asking us now to choose to take back our responsibility and stewardship over ourselves and our hearts.

This is an exercise in transferring the responsibility and stewardship of our life from other people or organizations into our own hands, regardless if someone else attempts to control us. No longer will we blame someone else for our poor decisions. We take back our life, taking responsibility for following God whether anyone else does or not.

<u>Step One</u>. Quiet yourself, focusing on Jesus, your Savior and Friend, or on Father God. You can begin by singing to Him about His goodness or praying and thanking Him.

<u>Step Two</u>. Ask the Father to show you any person or institution you rely upon or want to please more than Him—the One who made and loves you. You can pray something like this:

> *Dear Father, please reveal the truth to me no matter how uncomfortable it is. Please show me any person or thing that I put before You so I can take my responsibility for following and pleasing You. Amen (I agree).*

<u>Step Three</u>. Write down any thoughts that He shares with you. Hint: Do not be afraid that you are betraying someone you love by asking for truth because God's ultimate desire is to bless you and those whom you love. This is simply a truth-finding exercise. He will help you see the truth so you can be blessed to become a blessing (Genesis 12:2). He will make your way prosperous so you and those you love will have good success (Joshua 1:8). Let's trust Him!

____

____

____

____

____

____

<u>Step Four</u>. Once He shows you anything you have put before Him, pray something like this:

Dear Father (or Jesus), I turn from esteeming __________________ more than You. I choose to take responsibility for my life and to esteem You. I choose to follow You with my whole heart, regardless of who this connects me to or separates me from. I trust You to help me navigate any difficult situation I am in by seeing Your perspective more than my own or another's opinion. I trust You to take care of those I love because You love them more than I do. Amen (I agree).

Now that you have taken responsibility for your life, God will lead you more through your circumstances, relationships, and situations, and you will be a blessing to many. Write down all the changes and shifting He is doing inside your heart, both now and in the coming days, weeks, months, and years.

Additional Resources

The Bible – Various Translations
Keys to Freedom by Nancy Alcorn
The Bondage Breaker by Neil T. Anderson
Victory over Darkness by Neil T. Anderson
Steps to Freedom in Christ by Neil T. Anderson
Celebrate Recovery by John Baker
The Blood Covenant by E.W. Kenyon
Approval Addiction by Joyce Meyer
Healing The Orphaned Heart by Casey Treat
The Christian Codependence Recovery Workbook by Stephanie Trucker

Suggested Tips for Leaders

Atmosphere. Allow yourself 30 minutes for the leaders to pray before the participants arrive. Leaders should endeavor to be available to be led by the Lord as much as possible.

Structured Environment. Because a structured setting will ensure respect and dignity, the clearer the boundaries and rules are communicated and practiced, the safer the group. The safer the group feels, the more transparent it will be. The more transparent the group is, the more healing and bonding will happen. Boundaries and structure are therefore vital. To maintain structure and respect in the group, please follow group guidelines.

Table. Sitting around a table is preferred over sofa sitting. The atmosphere is not one of hanging out. This may seem confining in the beginning, but the implied boundaries and structure are important for participants to focus on themselves. Each participant should focus on their healing, life, and thoughts without focusing on the group. Remember, structure produces security.

Servant Leadership. Leaders are to facilitate each individual's healing through encouragement to connect with God and stay planted in the local church. For recovery, the leader's role is not to advise, teach, or correct doctrine or thinking. There are wonderful pastors and teachers who function in this role. Additionally, in this program, group leaders do not promote themselves or their ministries, functioning more as coaches who promote the success of athletes (participants).

Weekly Meeting Duration. Begin on time and leave on time. Start with prayer, weekly testimonies, the leader's encouragement to the group, and announcements (5-15 minutes). Move quickly into sharing time (80-100 minutes), which is the bulk of the meeting. For certain lessons, allow about 15 minutes at the end to lead the class into the Encounters. Close in prayer (5 minutes). In total, sessions will take approximately two hours.

Confidentiality. Of course, confidentiality is vital, not only for each participant but also for the leaders. Leaders do not discuss with other leaders anyone's story except if someone is in danger, for legal reasons, or until a participant has shared their story publicly. Recovery is messy. Just as a parent does not expose their child's messes but rather trains them up, likewise, we don't expose others' messes since participants are in the process. People are healing and changing rapidly during this program.

Sharing. To allow every person the opportunity to share, stay within the timeframe of sharing, and go in a circle. Do not utilize popcorn-style sharing. If a person does not want to share, they can simply pass.

- Watch for people who always pass and never participate. After a while, you will need to speak to them about why they are in the group.
- Keep people within the required time as much as possible without being rude.
- Help people stay focused on the question, and don't let them wander off too much.

Fellowship and Conversation. Community, accountability, friends, and prayer partners are encouraged before and after the group time.

- As much as possible, encourage small group accountability partners of three or four together, preferably not one-on-one.
- Watch for people who are in vulnerable positions so that a controlling personality does not attempt to dominate their time or life.

Diverse Doctrine or Theology. Although we don't wish to teach doctrine or theology, it is obvious that certain truths will produce these elements because this recovery program is going through the Bible. We are not here to argue any doctrine or push anything on anyone. The lessons are simply presented for the participant to choose to interact with or not. A leader's role is not to teach but to encourage and support each participant to connect personally with Jesus Christ through the written Word, action items, encounters, and meditations. We point each person to Him to resolve problems, find purpose, and heal brokenness.

Control. Control is not allowed. We are dealing with adults. Respect, honor, dignity, and free will are non-negotiables and should always be upheld even when we must confront poor behavior. This is not a job, club, or corporation.

- Having a strong structure removes the control from an individual and puts it onto the system or program, which everyone must be accountable to. Structure produces security.
- A participant is free to leave the group at any time without disapproval, judgement, or rejection from the group or leader. In the parable of the prodigal son, the father simply let the son go without chasing him.
- Not everyone is ready to self-assess. That does not make them evil. They belong to Him! Many people may drop off in the beginning, so do not take it personally. They usually come back for the next class.

Safety of the Group. Leaders are required to correct, warn, or remove anyone who violates another's space or safety, whether it be physical, emotional, psychological, or spiritual.

Inventory of Past Trauma. Although recovery can involve reviewing a past trauma or incident to allow the Holy Spirit to cleanse and heal a wound, leaders should never force anyone on such a journey. Of course, the Holy Spirit may lead a participant, leader, or group into these encounters, but it is never forced upon participants. *This process absolutely must be Holy Spirit led!*

Vocabulary. As leaders, try to keep the group from throwing out popular psychological terms that label them or each other. Although we don't want to correct people when they share, stay away from vocabulary that labels someone a certain way. Our only identity is that we are children of God, so no other label is necessary in this group. A good exercise is to look up definitions when people use catchphrases such as

- **Victim**: *Someone who has been violated.* It's also used in court cases along with plaintiff, defendant, victim, or judge and expresses one who was the recipient of a certain violation. It is not a lifelong position.
- **Brokenness**: *Something that does not work right or is unable to function as designed.* For this reason, we bring anything broken to the manufacturer (the Creator, God) for repair.
- **Recovery**: *To regain something that was lost.* This includes physical, mental, or relational health. Stay away from vocabulary that allows recovery to mean that we will never change or will always have the same problems. In this group, we actively pursue the goal of regaining what was lost.
- **Trauma**: *This is the Greek word for "wound."* Although historically it was used to describe something physical, in recent years, it is used to describe emotional wounds. In either case, the Great Physician, Jesus Christ, is available to us as the Healer, and we actively pursue healing of all wounds physically, mentally, emotionally, and spiritually.
- **Codependent**: *A complex word often described as a psychological condition*, which carries various behaviors—the most common being *unhealthy attachments*. In reality, this is the fallen condition of humanity after Adam and Eve lost their fellowship with God. Without Jesus, humanity has a gaping hole in their soul that they attempt to fill with various unhealthy attachments. Of course, the only remedy is accepting Jesus as Lord and Savior, allowing Him full access to our hearts. He becomes our healthy attachment!

Same-Gender Groups. Groups should not be mixed with men and women, nor should recovery groups be done between couples. At a minimum, transparency, safety, and security would be compromised. Furthermore, it opens the door to many issues.

Closed Group. This recovery program is designed for the same people to journey together from start to finish, which fosters a community of support and healthy accountability. After the second or third week, this group should be closed so that no new people can join or drop in. For this reason, it's a good idea to start another group every quarter so no one waits a whole year to join a group.

Avoid Family Members in the Same Group. If family members (e.g., mom and daughter, sisters, etc.) are in the same group, it will eventually reduce their experience from being transparent and honest. Optimum healing will be hindered. Even when we have good relationships with family members, it's best to come together *after* each member experiences their breakthrough, recovery, and healing journey with the Lord.

About the Author

Sharon Coletta is a wife and mother, which are her greatest passions. She was raised in a Catholic home and invited Jesus into her heart at the age of 21 while on an airplane en route to a college overseas exchange program. She graduated with a bachelor's degree in political science and a psychology minor, later joining the Peace Corps in Thailand. When she returned to the U.S., she attended Bible college. Because of her brief travels (including mission trips) in foreign countries, along with her studies, she has always viewed the gospel within a worldview of God's master plan on the earth: His story.

After Bible college, she held various roles on staff at Cottonwood Church. However, in 2010, she experienced a personally painful event that led her to a Celebrate Recovery class. Her personal journey to wholeness created an unyielding desire to see broken people healed, whole, and fulfilling their God-given purpose within His story. It was there that she learned many of the reasons people are the way they are and that God always has the remedy. Since then, she has led multiple recovery classes for women and worked with teenagers at a local runaway shelter.

In January 2023, while in corporate prayer at Oceans Church, God inspired her with the outline for *Made for His Glory*—a recovery journey that takes participants through the Bible as they heal. She continues to find great joy in coming alongside hurting and broken people who choose to allow God to heal, rebuild, and establish them in their God-given destiny and purpose.